AF668252

Greek Myths and Legends: A Modern Glimpse

Sabiya Kathiria

PEN

Manush

Title: Greek Myths and Legends: A Modern Glimpse

Author: Sabiya Kathiria

First Edition: 2025

ISBN: 9788198667342

Published by PENmanush under the Young Authorship Program – a platform that helps young writers become published authors.

www.penmanush.com | www.jyotsnabharti.com

AUTHOR'S NOTE

From a young age, I was always drawn to the glittering, opulent world of Greek gods and mythology. The *D'Aulaires' Book of Greek Mythology*, by Ingri d'Aulaire and Edgar Parin d'Aulaire, was a major inspiration for this book and my overall fascination with mythology. From the moment my 10-year-old hands opened that book in my school library, I was hooked. These stories continue to inspire and fuel creativity today: in paintings, movies, and literature. This book is a culmination of years of fascination with Greek mythology paired with a love of modern literature. I wanted to explore how the Gods' divine flaws mirror our lives centuries later. These stories reignite a childlike awe of enchantment, power, and fate; they let us believe, even for a second, that this magic remains around us, hidden, waiting to be uncovered.

You can connect with me on:

https://jyotsnabharti.com/sabiyakathiria/

Sabiya

CHAPTER 1
A Guide to the Gods

Zeus

At the apex of the Olympian pantheon stands Zeus, the king of the gods, sovereign of the sky, and wielder of thunder and lightning. He embodies authority, justice, and divine order, serving as both ruler of gods and arbiter of mortals. Zeus' power is unparalleled among the Olympians, and his presence dominates myth, literature, and religious practice in ancient Greece. Yet he is not merely a distant figure of authority; his personality is complex, blending wisdom, mercy, passion, and occasional caprice. To study Zeus is to confront the ideals of leadership, the dynamics of power, and the intricate relationships between authority, morality, and human experience.

Zeus' origins are steeped in cosmic drama. He is the youngest child of the Titans Cronus and Rhea, who, fearing a prophecy that he would be overthrown, swallowed each of his children at birth. Zeus was saved by his mother, hidden away on the island of

Crete, and eventually returned to challenge and defeat Cronus, freeing his siblings and establishing a new order of gods. This narrative reflects the central themes of Greek mythology: the struggle for power, the overturning of old authority, and the establishment of a just and enduring cosmic order. Zeus' rise to kingship represents not only physical might but also strategic cunning, foresight, and the moral authority to lead.

Zeus' myths emphasize both his supreme authority and his human-like characteristics. He governs the skies, controls the weather, and enforces oaths and justice, wielding the thunderbolt as a symbol of his unparalleled power. Yet Zeus is also famously involved in the affairs of mortals and gods alike, displaying desire, jealousy, and even temper. His numerous romantic escapades, and the offspring they produce, reflect the complexity of his character: he embodies divine power yet participates in the emotional and moral dramas that mirror human life. These stories illustrate the ancient Greeks' understanding that leadership and authority, even when divine, involve challenges, flaws, and ethical responsibilities.

Symbolically, Zeus represents order, governance,

and the maintenance of law and justice. He is the ultimate arbiter of morality, intervening when boundaries are broken or oaths are violated. Through Zeus, the Greeks explored themes of balance between power and responsibility, authority and restraint, as well as the delicate relationship between divine guidance and human agency. He is both a protector and a punisher, reflecting the dual nature of leadership: the capacity to nurture and to correct, to inspire loyalty and to enforce discipline.

In art, literature, and culture, Zeus is often depicted as a regal, bearded figure, holding a thunderbolt or seated on a throne, radiating strength and authority. His image conveys the ideals of leadership and justice, as well as the awe-inspiring presence of a deity who governs both the heavens and the earth. Festivals, temples, and oracles dedicated to Zeus—such as the grand sanctuary at Olympia—underscore his centrality in Greek religious and civic life. Worshipers looked to him not only for protection and guidance but also for the enforcement of moral and social order, recognizing the interdependence of divine authority and human society.

Modern storytellers continue to draw inspiration from Zeus' divine power, using his image to explore contemporary themes. "Zeus-like" is used by authors to describe a person with massive authority and power. Similarly, his thunderbolt remains an iconic symbol-in Rick Riordan's *Percy Jackson* series, Zeus and his thunderbolt remain iconic and prominent subjects in the plot.

Mary Shelley's *Frankenstein;* or, *The Modern Prometheus* provides one of the most enduring allusions to Zeus through the Prometheus myth. By casting Victor Frankenstein as a "modern Prometheus," Shelley indirectly invokes Zeus's punishment of Prometheus for stealing fire and giving it to humanity. Victor's relentless pursuit of knowledge and power mirrors Prometheus's defiance, while the tragic fallout reflects the consequences of challenging divine—or in this case, natural—limits set by a Zeus-like force.

Similarly, in Homer's *Iliad* and *Odyssey,* Zeus plays a vital role as the leader of the Olympians. His portrayal in this epic has been cemented into literature and continues to be important centuries later.

Aphrodite

A birth from sea foam. A scandalous affair with the god of war. A beauty so transcendent, she was proclaimed by Zeus himself to be the goddess of love and beauty.

The origins of Aphrodite are themselves a matter of mythic debate, mirroring her elusive and protean nature. In one tradition, she arises from the primordial violence of Uranus's downfall, born of sea foam and blood, carried by the tide until she reaches the shore of Cyprus. In another, she is counted among the Olympian children of Zeus, born of his union with Dione. The two versions tell us something essential: Aphrodite belongs to both heaven and earth, to the depths of the sea and the heights of Olympus. Her birth is not quiet or secondary—it is dramatic, charged with meaning, a reminder that love is never a tame or simple force, but one that bursts forth from strife and mystery.

The poets and artists of Greece lavished upon her an enduring attention. Homer spoke of her golden beauty, Hesiod named her as "foam-born," and later dramatists and sculptors rendered her presence in marble, bronze, and verse. Each portrayal speaks not only to her radiant allure but also to the weight of her influence. To the ancients, beauty was never merely decoration; it was a form of power, a sway over hearts and destinies. Aphrodite is the keeper of that power, embodying its blessings and its dangers alike. She could bless marriages and make gardens bloom, yet she could also incite jealousy, rivalry, and war—the most famous instance being the spark she lit for the Trojan War when she promised Paris the most beautiful woman in the world.

Her mythology, rich and varied, makes her a paradoxical figure. She is the goddess who unites lovers, yet she herself is entangled in endless affairs, bound to Hephaestus yet passionately drawn to Ares, and ever accompanied by Eros, the winged god of desire. She is the gentle patroness of courtesans and poets, yet also a cunning manipulator of kings and heroes. She represents the tenderest embrace and the fiercest longing, a reminder that love is not merely sweetness—it is also fire.

Aphrodite's presence was not confined to myth alone; it permeated the daily lives of the Greeks and Romans. Temples rose in her honor, from the shores of Cyprus to the hills of Corinth, where her cult thrived. Offerings of perfume, flowers, and doves adorned her altars. Sailors prayed to her for safe passage, lovers for fidelity, brides for fertility. Her Roman counterpart, Venus, inherited and extended her influence, becoming not just a goddess of desire but a guardian of the empire, linked to the founding myths of Rome itself. In every guise, she reveals how profoundly the ancients saw beauty and desire as forces shaping both private life and public destiny.

To study Aphrodite, then, is to study the eternal question of love's place in human life. She is the embodiment of our yearning for connection, our awe before beauty, and our vulnerability to passion. She is as present in the flicker of a modern romance as she was in the hymns of ancient Greece, as visible in art galleries and poetry books today as in temples two thousand years ago. More than a goddess, Aphrodite is an idea; one that reminds us that love is not merely an ornament of life but its very heartbeat, capable of both healing and harm.

Even today, to be called an "Aphroditean beauty" is a compliment of the highest regard, invoking the timeless ideal of love and beauty that the goddess represents. Her companion, Cupid, has become a universal symbol of romance, particularly visible during Valentine's Day, where his image decorates cards, candies, and merchandise in department stores around the world. Artistic masterpieces such as Botticelli's *The Birth of Venus,* which depicts Aphrodite rising from the sea, remain some of the most celebrated works in Western art, reproduced and reinterpreted countless times for their elegance and cultural resonance. Beyond high art, Aphrodite's presence also lingers in popular culture: teenagers dress up as her for Halloween, donning Greek goddess costumes, while fashion, film, and music frequently reference her as a symbol of allure and empowerment. From fine art to consumer holidays to modern self-expression, Aphrodite endures as a cultural icon, embodying the intersection of beauty, love, and desire in both classical and contemporary contexts.

Poseidon

Commander of the seas, storms, and all aquatic realms, earning him the title of god of the oceans, earthquakes, and horses. He is one of the most powerful deities of Greek mythology, second only to his brother Zeus in might, yet his influence is distinct, unpredictable, and elemental. Poseidon embodies the raw, untamed forces of nature—the power that can nourish, protect, and awe, but also destroy and terrify. To invoke Poseidon is to confront both the grandeur and the danger of the natural world, and to acknowledge the necessity of respect, caution, and humility in the face of forces beyond human control.

Poseidon's origins are steeped in divine lineage. He is the son of the Titans Cronus and Rhea, and brother to Zeus and Hades. Alongside his siblings, Poseidon overthrew Cronus to claim his share of power in the new Olympian order. Unlike Zeus, whose domain is the sky, or Hades, ruler of the underworld, Poseidon claims the vast and unpredictable oceans, along with the creatures within them and the land shaken by his trident. His authority is immense but unstable, reflecting the inherent volatility of water itself—capable of serenity and life-giving abundance, yet equally capable of fury and destruction.

Poseidon's myths reveal his dual nature: he is both protector and punisher, a deity whose moods mirror the seas he governs. Sailors and coastal communities depended on his favor for safe passage, offering sacrifices and prayers to avoid storms or shipwreck. At the same time, Poseidon could unleash devastating tempests, floods, or earthquakes in response to disrespect or defiance, demonstrating that power, though magnificent, carries responsibility and consequences. He is also associated with horses and horsemanship, symbolizing vitality, freedom, and strength, while highlighting his connection to land as well as sea.

Symbolically, Poseidon embodies the untamed, elemental forces of nature, the unpredictability of life, and the necessity of respect for the world beyond human control. His trident, often depicted in art and literature, is a symbol of his capacity to create and destroy, to stabilize and disrupt, emphasizing the duality of power. Poseidon's temperament and actions reflect the understanding that natural forces are neither inherently benevolent nor malevolent, but must be approached with reverence, intelligence, and adaptability.

Poseidon is *the* integral figure in Rick Riordan's renowned *Percy Jackson* series. Poseidon's son in the novels, Percy, is loved by readers across the globe. Disney and Fox have both adapted the Greek Myth-inspired book series into a TV-show and movie, respectively. Poseidon's role as God of the Seas quite literally inspired the entire series–his relevance is apparent even in young adult books.

Demeter

The goddess of agriculture, fertility, and the cycles of life and death. She is the divine nurturer, the provider of sustenance, and the protector of the harvest, whose power ensures the survival of both mortals and gods. Through her dominion over the earth's bounty, Demeter embodies the essential rhythms of nature: growth, decay, and renewal. Her influence stretches far beyond the simple act of planting and harvesting; she represents the intimate connection between humans and the natural world, the interdependence of life, and the sacredness of the cycles that sustain existence.

Demeter's origins place her among the most ancient and revered of the Olympians. She is the daughter of Cronus and Rhea, making her a sister of Zeus, Hera, Hestia, Hades, and Poseidon. From the beginning, Demeter is linked to the fundamental needs of humanity: the cultivation of grain, the fertility of the land, and the continuity of life through seasonal cycles. Her authority reflects the recognition that survival depends not only on strength or intellect, but on care, patience, and reverence for the natural world. Demeter's power is life-sustaining, and her absence or displeasure can have catastrophic consequences, a truth immortalized in myth and ritual.

Central to Demeter's mythology is the story of her daughter, Persephone, whose abduction by Hades brings forth the seasons. In her grief, Demeter withdraws her gifts from the earth, causing famine and despair among mortals. This myth explains the natural cycle of growth and dormancy, illustrating the deep connection between human life and the divine forces of nature. It also highlights Demeter's emotional depth and maternal devotion: her love for Persephone drives her actions, revealing the goddess as both nurturing and fiercely protective. Through this story, the Greeks conveyed profound truths about loss, renewal, and the interdependence of life and death, making Demeter a deity whose power is both practical and deeply symbolic.

Demeter's role extends beyond mythology into the spiritual and civic life of the Greeks. She was worshiped in festivals such as the Eleusinian Mysteries, one of the most important religious rites in ancient Greece, which promised initiates understanding of life, death, and rebirth. These rituals celebrated the cycles of nature, the promise of renewal, and the sacred relationship between humans and the earth. Demeter's presence in these ceremonies underscores her role as a mediator between mortality and divinity, a bridge between the physical and spiritual sustenance that humans require.

Symbolically, Demeter represents the enduring forces of life, growth, and continuity. She is a reminder that human survival depends on care, patience, and respect for the natural order, and that the cycles of fertility and decay are not merely agricultural phenomena but reflections of the broader rhythms of existence. Her character embodies maternal devotion, resilience, and the quiet yet unstoppable power of nurture. Unlike deities associated with conquest or passion, Demeter wields her influence through provision, protection, and the sustaining power of life itself.

In art and literature, Demeter is often depicted with sheaves of wheat, cornucopias, or a torch—symbols of nourishment, guidance, and fertility. Her image evokes both the abundance of the earth and the emotional depth of maternal love, combining practical sustenance with moral and spiritual significance. Through Demeter, the Greeks articulated a vision of life as a balance between giving and receiving, nurturing and respecting, growth and decay.

Athena

Among the pantheon of Greek gods and goddesses, Athena stands as a figure of unparalleled intellect, courage, and strategic mastery. She is the goddess of wisdom, war, and crafts, a deity whose influence bridges both the cerebral and the martial, the contemplative and the active. Athena embodies a balance that the ancients revered: the harmony of thought and action, reason and strength, logic and justice. She is not merely a goddess of warfare, like Ares, who embodies raw violence and chaos; Athena represents the disciplined, tactical application of force, the art of strategy, and the pursuit of knowledge. To invoke her name is to summon the ideals of wisdom and the nobility of rational power.

The origins of Athena are as extraordinary as her character. According to myth, she was born fully grown and armored from the head of Zeus, the king of the gods, after he experienced a great headache. This miraculous birth symbolizes her intimate connection with intellect and reason: she emerges directly from the mind, not the womb, embodying wisdom in its purest form. Athena's birth, sudden and awe-inspiring, set her apart from other deities. She would not be defined by desire or passion but by intellect, skill, and the pursuit of justice. Her presence in Greek mythology underscores the idea that strength guided by wisdom is far more formidable than brute force alone.

Athena's myths and stories reveal the complexity of her character. She was the patroness of heroes, guiding Odysseus through cunning strategies, shielding Perseus in his quest against Medusa, and supporting Heracles in his labors. She embodies mentorship, foresight, and moral judgment, demonstrating that true power often lies in guidance and foresight rather than in domination. At the same time, Athena is associated with crafts, especially weaving and pottery, representing human creativity and skill. She is both a warrior and an artisan, a symbol of civilization and intellect, showing that the Greek understanding of wisdom was holistic, encompassing both thought and craft.

Athena's symbolic role extended into the heart of Greek culture and civic life. She was the patron deity of Athens, the city that bears her name, where she was revered not only for her protective power but also as the embodiment of the city's ideals: democracy, learning, and civic pride. The Parthenon, her magnificent temple atop the Acropolis, was a testament to her central place in Greek society. Citizens offered sacrifices and tributes to her, seeking guidance in both public affairs and private endeavors. Athena's wisdom was seen as essential to governance, strategy, and the pursuit of justice, and her figure represented the ideal citizen: thoughtful, courageous, and capable of contributing meaningfully to the polis.

Athena's personality in myth also reflects a disciplined moral code. Unlike many gods who act on whim or passion, she is measured, strategic, and principled. She rewards intelligence, courage, and diligence, while punishing hubris and reckless violence. Athena's temper is calm but formidable; she can guide and protect, yet those who act foolishly or dishonorably are met with her stern justice. Her embodiment of reason, strategy, and virtue makes her a model not only for heroes but also for the human aspiration toward wisdom and ethical action.

In Rick Riordan's *Percy Jackson and the Olympians* series, Athena's influence is most strongly felt through her daughter, Annabeth Chase. Annabeth embodies her mother's qualities of wisdom, intelligence, and strategic thinking, often serving as the planner and voice of reason among Percy's group. Her character makes Athena's legacy accessible to a modern YA audience, reshaping the goddess not just as a distant mythological figure, but as an enduring archetype of intellect and problem-solving that remains vital in stories of heroism today.

Madeline Miller's *Circe* offers another perspective on Athena's relevance in modern literature. While the novel centers on the witch Circe, Athena plays a significant role as a figure of divine authority, embodying the tension between mortal autonomy and divine control.

Her interactions with Circe highlight Athena's traditional domains—wisdom, strategy, and influence—but also cast her in a critical light, as

Miller uses Athena to explore themes of power, freedom, and the cost of resistance. In this way, Athena's presence serves as a reminder that wisdom can also be wielded as dominance, a concept that resonates with contemporary readers attuned to questions of authority and self-determination.

In popular culture, Athena's archetype has deeply shaped the portrayal of Wonder Woman in DC Comics. While Diana Prince is not Athena herself, she is often depicted as having been blessed by the goddess and draws heavily from Athena's attributes. Wonder Woman embodies both martial prowess and intellectual strength, demonstrating that true heroism comes from the balance of mind and body. Through this connection, Athena's influence permeates one of the most iconic superheroes of the modern age, cementing her as a symbol of justice, wisdom, and female empowerment.

Athena's cultural impact also extends beyond literature and film into branding and symbolism. Her association with wisdom and strategy makes her image a popular emblem for institutions and companies seeking to project intelligence, trust, and authority. The owl of Athena, for example, frequently appears in academic contexts, from university seals to honor societies, while businesses across industries—from health care to consulting—use her name to signify reliability and knowledge. These uses demonstrate how Athena's identity has transcended mythology to become a universal shorthand for intellect and strength in contemporary culture.

Hera

Among the Olympian deities, Hera stands as a figure of regal authority, unwavering dignity, and commanding presence. She is the goddess of marriage, family, and women, revered as the protector of unions and the sanctity of domestic life. Yet Hera is far more than a domestic figure; she embodies power, sovereignty, and an unshakable will, commanding respect and often demanding justice. To invoke Hera is to summon the ideals of loyalty, commitment, and the moral and social structures that sustain civilization. She represents the order and stability that allow both gods and mortals to flourish within the bonds of family and society.

Hera's origins place her among the most powerful of the Olympians. She is the daughter of Cronus and Rhea, making her a sister of Zeus, Poseidon, and Hades. Despite this shared lineage, Hera's mythic narrative is defined by her union with Zeus, her brother and the king of the gods, which cements her position as queen of Olympus. However, her marriage is famously tumultuous, marked by Zeus's infidelities and Hera's responses of jealousy, cunning, and retribution. These stories, while sometimes portraying her as vengeful, also highlight her role as the guardian of marital fidelity and social order. Hera's narrative illustrates the tension between personal loyalty and the challenges of power, reflecting the complexities of human relationships in divine form.

Hera's myths reveal both her strengths and her depth of character. She is often portrayed as a formidable figure, capable of influencing the fates of gods and mortals alike. Her interventions are motivated by a sense of justice and an insistence on respect for marriage and societal norms. Hera punishes wrongdoing, particularly acts of betrayal or hubris, yet she also rewards loyalty and devotion. She is the protector of women in their roles as wives and mothers, offering guidance and aid in times of need. In this way, Hera embodies the tension between compassion and authority, nurturing and power, making her a goddess of profound moral and social significance.

Hera's symbolic role extends beyond her personal narratives into the very structure of Greek society. As the goddess of marriage, she was honored in festivals such as the Heraia, and temples across Greece were dedicated to her worship. Her presence reinforced the ideals of family, loyalty, and societal cohesion, offering both divine protection and moral instruction. In art and literature, Hera is often depicted as majestic and commanding, adorned with a crown and scepter, symbolizing her status as queen of the gods. Her authority is both maternal and sovereign, representing the dual power of nurture and governance.

Yet Hera's personality in mythology is complex and multifaceted. She is strong, assertive, and sometimes feared, but her actions are grounded in principles of justice, fidelity, and respect for the divine and social order. Unlike gods who act solely on impulse or passion, Hera's decisions are measured and purposeful, reflecting the weight of her responsibilities. She demonstrates that true power is not merely physical or magical, but rooted in authority, wisdom, and moral conviction. Hera teaches that leadership and influence require courage, vigilance, and an unwavering commitment to principles.

In essence, Hera embodies the enduring human values of loyalty, responsibility, and social order. She reminds mortals and gods alike that love and marriage are not solely matters of desire but of duty, respect, and ethical commitment. Her influence extends beyond the myths of ancient Greece, inspiring representations of feminine strength, moral authority, and sovereign power throughout literature, art, and culture.

Hera's counterpart in Roman mythology is Juno. The name *Juno* is thought to be connected to the Latin word *iuvenis,* meaning "youth" or "vital force." This connection ties Juno to vitality, renewal, and fertility—traits that reflect her role as protector of women, childbirth, and the Roman state. Modern pop culture still draws on these associations, even in works that may not consciously reference mythology. For example, the movie *Juno* (2007), directed by Jason Reitman, follows a teenage girl navigating an unplanned pregnancy. While comedic in tone, the film ultimately explores themes of fertility, resilience, and the transition into womanhood—qualities that resonate with Juno's mythological domain. Similarly, Sabrina Carpenter's recent song "Juno" uses the name as a symbol of vitality, sexuality, and freedom, celebrating feminine power and autonomy. Both examples demonstrate how the name Juno, and by extension Hera, continues to embody enduring ideas of womanhood, strength, and renewal in contemporary culture.

Apollo and Artemis

Among the Olympian deities, few divine siblings are as intertwined yet as distinct in their powers, personalities, and symbolic significance as Apollo and Artemis. Children of Zeus and Leto, born under extraordinary circumstances due to the wrath of Hera, they embody complementary aspects of life, nature, and human experience. Apollo, the radiant god of the sun, music, prophecy, and healing, represents illumination, intellect, and harmony, while Artemis, the moon goddess of the hunt, wilderness, and chastity, embodies independence, protection, and the raw, untamed forces of nature. Together, they form a duality that balances light and dark, civilization and wilderness, order and instinct, reflecting the full spectrum of divine and human existence.

Apollo's origins and powers reflect his role as a god of rationality, creativity, and foresight. Born on the island of Delos, he grew to embody the ideals of Greek beauty, harmony, and intelligence. Often depicted with a lyre, laurel wreath, or bow, Apollo is a patron of the arts, especially music and poetry, highlighting the transformative and civilizing power of culture. His prophetic abilities, channeled through the Oracle of Delphi, made him a god whose influence reached far beyond mere aesthetics; he shaped human decisions, warned of danger, and revealed the hidden truths of the future. Apollo represents the radiant clarity of reason and vision, the guiding light that illuminates both the world of mortals and the mysteries of the divine.

Yet Apollo's character is far from one-dimensional. While he embodies reason, beauty, and order, he also has a fierce and sometimes destructive side. He wields the power to bring plague and death, demonstrating that divine authority is both a gift and a responsibility. His myths, ranging from the pursuit of the nymph Daphne to his conflicts with the satyr Marsyas, reveal the dangers of hubris, unbridled desire, and moral failings. Through Apollo, the Greeks explored the interplay between intellect and emotion, discipline and passion, showing that even the god of light is bound by the consequences of human-like desires and divine power.

Artemis, Apollo's twin sister, embodies a contrasting but complementary energy: the wild, protective, and fiercely independent. She is the goddess of the hunt, the wilderness, and the moon, representing a power untethered to civilization, yet deeply connected to life and nature. Like Apollo, she was born under extraordinary circumstances, and from an early age, she claimed independence and authority. Artemis is often depicted with a bow and quiver, surrounded by animals, highlighting her role as a guardian of wildlife and the natural world. She is also a protector of young women, particularly during the vulnerable transitions of childhood and adolescence, asserting the importance of safety, autonomy, and dignity.

Artemis' mythology frequently emphasizes her strict moral code and unwavering independence. She is the goddess of chastity, choosing to remain unbound by romantic attachment, and punishes those who violate sacred laws or threaten her domain. At the same time, she embodies nurturing qualities, healing, and protection, particularly for women and children, revealing the duality of her character as both fierce warrior and compassionate guardian. Through Artemis, the Greeks explored themes of autonomy, feminine power, and the tension between wildness and civilization, presenting a model of divinity that exists outside conventional domestic or romantic roles.

The duality of Apollo and Artemis extends beyond their individual powers to the symbolic balance they represent together. Apollo's dominion over the sun, light, and culture contrasts with Artemis' command of the moon, night, and wilderness, reflecting the natural cycles and dualities of life: day and night, reason and instinct, order and chaos. Their complementary roles underscore the Greek understanding of harmony and balance, suggesting that wisdom and intuition, civilization and nature, must coexist for the world to flourish. Both deities exert influence over human morality, guiding mortals through both inspiration and restraint, illuminating the ethical and emotional dimensions of human life.

Apollo and Artemis also shaped the cultural, religious, and civic life of the ancient Greeks. Apollo's oracles, temples, and festivals, such as the Pythian Games at Delphi, celebrated music, prophecy, and athletic skill, encouraging excellence and reverence for divine guidance. Artemis was honored through rituals emphasizing protection, fertility, and the sanctity of nature, such as the Brauronia festival for young girls in Athens. Through these cultic practices, both gods influenced the daily lives of mortals, shaping civic identity, personal ethics, and the early human evaluation of natural and supernatural forces.

Hephaestus

Among the Olympian gods, Hephaestus stands apart as the divine embodiment of craftsmanship, ingenuity, and transformative labor. Unlike deities of war, love, or the hunt, Hephaestus is the god of fire, metalworking, sculpture, and invention. He is the master artisan of Olympus, the divine smith whose hands shape not only the weapons and tools of gods and heroes but also the very essence of human creativity. While he may not possess the immediate allure of Aphrodite or the radiant intellect of Athena, Hephaestus' power lies in his ability to create, to transform raw material into objects of beauty, utility, and sometimes unimaginable force. He represents the quiet, steady force of human skill, perseverance, and the sacred act of making.

Hephaestus' origins are as complex as his character. In some myths, he is the son of Hera alone, born without a father, while in others he is the child of both Hera and Zeus. His birth is marked by imperfection and rejection: he was said to be born lame or physically deformed, and in some stories, Hera cast him from Olympus in shame. This origin story establishes Hephaestus as a figure who embodies resilience and defiance, a god who transforms marginalization into mastery. His physical imperfection contrasts sharply with the beauty and perfection of the objects he creates, symbolizing the idea that true genius and value often emerge from struggle, labor, and perseverance.

Hephaestus' myths reveal the depth of his intellect, skill, and moral complexity. He forged some of the most legendary artifacts of Greek mythology, including Achilles' armor, Hermes' winged helmet and sandals, and the fateful chains that bound

Prometheus. His workshop, often imagined as a fiery cavern beneath a volcano, is both a place of creation and a realm of power, where sparks and molten metal become instruments of both protection and vengeance. Hephaestus' artistry demonstrates the divine capacity to bring order, function, and beauty out of chaos and raw material, echoing the human pursuit of mastery over the natural world.

Yet Hephaestus is also deeply human in his experiences and emotions. He is married to Aphrodite, a union fraught with tension, desire, and betrayal, illustrating the interplay of love, jealousy, and pride. In some myths, he uses his craft as a means of asserting his agency and exacting justice, as when he traps Aphrodite and Ares in an unbreakable net to expose their affair to the gods. Through these stories, Hephaestus embodies themes of resilience, intelligence, and the subtle exertion of power.

His genius is never brute; it is patient, precise, and calculated, revealing a form of authority rooted not in physical might or beauty, but in intellect, skill, and ingenuity.

Symbolically, Hephaestus represents the transformative power of work, invention, and persistence. He is a patron of artisans, blacksmiths, and engineers, and his influence extends to every human endeavor that involves making, shaping, and refining. Unlike gods associated with fleeting emotion or external appearance, Hephaestus reminds mortals that enduring power lies in creation and mastery of craft. He transforms fire—an element of danger and destruction—into instruments of civilization, art, and protection, reflecting the Greek reverence for skill, labor, and intelligence applied with purpose.

In art and culture, Hephaestus is depicted with the tools of his trade: hammer, tongs, and anvil, often surrounded by fire and molten metal. His physical imperfections are juxtaposed with the perfection of his creations, emphasizing that genius and value emerge not from superficial qualities, but from skill, dedication, and vision. Hephaestus teaches that mastery is earned through discipline and labor, that true power can be subtle and constructive, and that human ingenuity mirrors divine creativity.

Ares

Unique and often controversial among the Gods. As the god of war, violence, and bloodshed, he embodies the raw, chaotic, and destructive aspects of conflict. Unlike Athena, who represents strategy, wisdom, and disciplined combat, Ares is the personification of war's passion, fury, and primal force. He represents the visceral, untamed side of human aggression—the instinctual drive to fight, dominate, and assert power. While his role may seem violent or even frightening, it reflects a crucial dimension of both human nature and mythology: the recognition that conflict is an inseparable, and sometimes necessary, aspect of life.

Ares' origins are as distinguished as they are consequential. He is the son of Zeus and Hera, born into the power and authority of Olympus, yet his character sharply contrasts with the measured rule of his parents.

Hera and Zeus themselves represent law, order, and sovereignty, but in Ares, their progeny manifests the disruptive energy that can challenge peace, provoke fear, and test courage. In myth, Ares is often associated with bloodshed on the battlefield, yet he is not merely a god of chaos; he is a force that compels mortals and gods alike to confront their strength, resilience, and moral limits.

Ares' myths illustrate both his strengths and his limitations. He is a fierce warrior, unyielding in combat, and unafraid to confront even the most formidable opponents. Yet he is often portrayed as impulsive, quarrelsome, and susceptible to defeat, emphasizing the dangers of unchecked aggression and the consequences of acting without wisdom or restraint. In stories of the Trojan War, for instance, Ares participates in the brutal clashes between mortals and gods, reveling in combat, but he is also wounded, humiliated, or outmaneuvered by the cleverness of Athena. These narratives underscore a dual message: war requires courage, yet valor alone is insufficient without discipline, strategy, and ethical guidance.

Symbolically, Ares represents the intense, primal aspects of human nature that civilization seeks to regulate: anger, desire for dominance, courage, and the willingness to engage in conflict when necessary. He embodies the recognition that aggression is neither inherently good nor evil—it is a force that must be understood, directed, and, ideally, tempered by reason and morality. Ares' presence reminds mortals that conflict is inevitable, that violence carries consequences, and that mastery of one's instincts is essential to achieving both personal and societal balance.

In art and culture, Ares is often depicted as a muscular, armed warrior, sometimes bloodied or in the throes of battle, reflecting his embodiment of raw force and martial energy. His Roman counterpart, Mars, would later be celebrated more positively as a symbol of military honor and protection of the state, highlighting a cultural shift from fear and chaos toward structured and principled martial valor. Yet even in Greek tradition, Ares' complex nature—simultaneously feared, respected, and often scorned—emphasizes that the gods reflect not only idealized virtues but also the challenges, instincts, and imperfections inherent in human life.

Ultimately, Ares is a god who confronts humanity with its most primal and unrestrained impulses. He is a reminder that conflict, courage, and aggression are inseparable from life, and that understanding and managing these forces is part of the human condition.

Hermes

A deity of travel, commerce, communication, and cunning. Son of Zeus and the nymph Maia, Hermes embodies agility, wit, and versatility. He moves freely between worlds—Olympus, the mortal realm, and the underworld—bridging gaps and delivering messages, guiding souls, and facilitating trade and negotiation.

Hermes' mythology emphasizes his intelligence and resourcefulness. From his earliest myths, he is depicted as inventive and mischievous, famously stealing Apollo's cattle as an infant and inventing the lyre to appease him. He is both a trickster and a helper, using his cleverness to achieve goals, resolve conflicts, and assist heroes. In doing so, he represents adaptability, ingenuity, and the power of intellect over brute force.

Symbolically, Hermes embodies communication, transition, and the movement of ideas, goods, and people. His winged sandals, caduceus, and hat mark him as a god of speed and connection, guiding mortals and gods alike. Unlike gods tied to strength or beauty, Hermes' influence lies in agility, cunning, and cleverness, qualities that shape human interaction, commerce, and exploration.

In essence, Hermes is the divine guide and communicator, a god of movement, trade, and intellect. He reminds mortals that wit, adaptability, and resourcefulness are as powerful as strength, inspiring creativity, cleverness, and the pursuit of knowledge in every sphere of life.

Dionysus

Wine, ecstasy, theater, and transformation. Representing both the liberating and chaotic forces of human experience, he is the god of celebration and frenzy, yet also of introspection, madness, and renewal. Born of Zeus and the mortal Semele, Dionysus embodies the intersection of divinity and humanity, mortality and immortality, reflecting the complex dualities of life: pleasure and suffering, freedom and restraint, chaos and order.

Dionysus' mythology emphasizes his role as both disruptor and healer. He introduces wine to humanity, a substance that can bring joy, creativity, and social cohesion, but also excess, recklessness, and instability. He travels widely, spreading his cult and challenging traditional social norms, liberating followers from inhibitions and rigid structures. His followers, often including women known as Maenads, partake in ecstatic rituals that dissolve boundaries, illustrating the god's power to transform consciousness and break the constraints of ordinary life.

Symbolically, Dionysus embodies the essential tension between civilization and instinct, control and abandon. He represents the necessity of emotional release, artistic expression, and the acknowledgment of life's irrational, unpredictable dimensions. Unlike gods of reason or war, Dionysus' power is subtle, psychological, and spiritual, operating through inspiration, revelry, and transformation rather than force.

In art and literature, Dionysus is depicted as both youthful and effeminate, often crowned with ivy, holding a thyrsus or cup of wine, surrounded by satyrs and Maenads. These images convey both his seductive allure and the wildness of his influence, reflecting the dual capacity to delight and disrupt. Dionysus' myths emphasize the profound human need for ecstasy, creativity, and connection to forces beyond logic or control.

Ultimately, Dionysus embodies the liberating and transformative aspects of life. He reminds mortals that joy and chaos, pleasure and danger, artistry and instinct are inseparable dimensions of existence. As the god of wine, theater, and spiritual ecstasy, Dionysus celebrates the vitality of life, the necessity of emotional release, and the power of transformation, leaving a lasting legacy in both ancient mythology and modern cultural imagination.

CHAPTER 2

The Original Hero's Journey

The Hero's Journey, first conceptualized by Joseph Campbell in *The Hero with a Thousand Faces* (1949), outlines a universal pattern seen across myths, legends, and epic stories around the world. This "monomyth," as Campbell called it, follows a distinct arc: the hero begins in the ordinary world, receives a call to adventure, faces trials and temptations, meets mentors and allies, undergoes a major ordeal, claims a reward, and returns transformed. Though this structure is traditionally applied to male heroes like Hercules, Perseus, or Odysseus, Greek mythology actually contains far more nuance. When we look beyond the obvious, we see that women, antiheroes, and even groups play just as vital a role in shaping these mythic narratives—challenging the linear, male-centric path we've come to expect from hero stories. This chapter seeks to reimagine the Hero's Journey by centering different kinds of protagonists and journeys found within Greek mythology.

Classical Greek myths often showcase male demigods who follow the monomyth to near perfection. Hercules (or Herakles) is the textbook example. His Twelve Labors mirror Campbell's stages almost exactly: his call to adventure comes when he is ordered to complete impossible tasks; his trials involve facing monsters like the Nemean lion and the Hydra; he experiences death and rebirth during his descent into the underworld; and eventually he is granted immortality. Similarly, Odysseus's long journey home in *The Odyssey* tracks with the Hero's Journey, including supernatural aid (Athena), tests (the Cyclops, the Sirens), and ultimate transformation. However, focusing only on these examples limits our understanding of what a hero can be.

Greek mythology offers many female figures who, while not traditionally seen as "heroes," follow arcs that are just as epic and transformative—though often more tragic, complex, or collective in nature. Take *Atalanta*, for example, a huntress raised by bears who refused to marry unless a suitor could beat her in a footrace. Though she is eventually tricked by Hippomenes with the help of Aphrodite, Atalanta's journey is still one of agency, independence, and struggle against societal expectations of women. Her heroism isn't defined by conquest, but by resistance. Similarly, *Medea*, often cast as a villain, can be seen as an antihero: she aids Jason in completing his quest, betrays her family for love, and then is betrayed in return—leading to her vengeful and horrifying actions. Medea doesn't follow the Hero's Journey to achieve honor or glory. Instead, her story shows what happens when a character is forced into the margins of power and responds with rage, making her a mythological antihero long before the term existed.

Even collective journeys in Greek myth challenge the lone-hero structure. The Argonauts , for example, embark on their quest as a group led by Jason, but the success of their voyage depends on the collaboration of many different individuals with unique skills—Orpheus, Heracles, Atalanta, and others. Unlike Hercules' solo trials, the Argonauts' journey emphasizes teamwork and mutual reliance. Similarly, the women of The Bacchae (in Euripides' play) experience a collective transformation when they reject the rigid structures of Thebes under

Dionysus's influence. Their journey is less about physical adventure and more about psychological and spiritual awakening—still fitting within Campbell's framework, but with a collective twist.

By reimagining the Hero's Journey in the context of Greek mythology, we can see that the structure is not as rigid or male-dominated as it appears at first glance. Female figures like Atalanta and Medea, though often misunderstood, carve out heroic paths defined by agency, intellect, and emotional depth. Antiheroes disrupt the moral clarity of the monomyth, exposing the darker undercurrents of power, betrayal, and revenge. Collective journeys, meanwhile, challenge the idea that one individual must carry the weight of destiny alone. These reimaginings don't discard Campbell's framework but expand it, showing that the journey toward transformation can take many forms—not just the muscular, monster-slaying path of Hercules. Greek mythology is the original Hero's Journey, exemplifying the archetype of the iconic hero.

CHAPTER 3

The Man, The Myth, The Legend

Mythology evokes attention and endless praise because its stories humanize and strip down the hero into an everyday man. Mythical men are flawed but extraordinary, with the authors of Myth plucking traits of the regular man and creating a vicariously delicious blend of heroism and reality. In this way, myth allows its protagonists to transcend the traditional hero archetype–it celebrates human error instead of erasing it entirely.

Hercules was born out of an affair Zeus had with a mortal woman, Alcmene. When Hera discovered that Zeus' infidelity had bred a child, she was overcome with jealousy and hatred for the child. Hera sent snakes to strangle Hercules as a child, but with his strength and bravery, Hercules easily fought them off.

Eventually, Hercules grew into a powerful warrior–as he was a demigod, Hercules was unusually strong and fearless. After helping Creon, the king of Thebes, drive invaders away, he was offered the King's eldest daughter, Megara. The two were happily married and had three sons.

Driven by her jealousy, Hera once again planned to hurt Hercules. She sent Lyssa, the god of madness, to drive Hercules insane. In a tragic and heightened fit of rage and insanity, Hercules murdered his wife, Megara, and three children. This eventually led Hercules to atone for his sins through his famous 12 labors.

Achilles was known to be the greatest of all Greek warriors as the son of a King and a pupil of Chiron, the centaur who taught Hercules. While fighting in the Trojan War, Achilles becomes deeply offended when King Argemmon, the Greek commander, steals Briseis, whom Achilles valued as a war prize. Insulted and enraged, Achilles withdraws from battle, leading the Greeks to face massive losses in war. As the Greeks suffer endlessly and cruelly, Patroclus, Achilles' best friend and possible lover, begs Achilles to fight in a futile attempt to save the Greek soldiers. Achilles refuses, as his pride blinds him from doing the honorable thing and saving his men. Patroclus takes Achilles' armor, knowing that the mere sight of the great warrior will be enough to encourage the Greek troops and push back the Trojans. He is tragically killed in battle by Hector, prince of Troy–a direct consequence of Achilles' pride and ego.

After Patroclus dies, Achilles murders Hector in bitter vengeance, refusing to return Hector's body to his family for a proper burial. Instead, he desecrates it, dragging it around and treats the body with such cruelty that even shocks the gods. When Hector's old father begs Achilles for mercy over Hector's body, Achilles finally breaks down and returns it.

Achilles' story–his refusal to fight and blind rage–demonstrates a common theme in Greek texts: **Hubris**, excessive pride and arrogance. Similar to how Icarus flew too close to the sun, Achilles went overboard with his display of ego, leading to not his own death, but the death of the one he loved the most.

CHAPTER 4
A Tale of Two Foes

Among the countless tales of the Greek pantheon, few rivalries capture the essence of divine competition as vividly as that of Athena and Poseidon. The goddess of wisdom and strategy, and the god of the sea and earthquakes, clashed in a contest that was as much about power and prestige as it was about human civilization and its ideals. Their rivalry, most famously depicted in the contest over the city of Athens, reflects deeper themes of intellect versus instinct, order versus raw power, and strategic foresight versus brute force—concepts that resonate far beyond the mythic landscape of ancient Greece.

The story begins with the founding of Athens, a city destined for greatness under the gaze of the gods. Both Athena and Poseidon desired to become its patron deity. To prove their worth, each offered a gift to the city. Poseidon struck the ground with his trident, producing a spring or saltwater pool—a source of power and potential naval dominance.

Athena, in contrast, planted an olive tree, providing sustenance, oil, and wood—an enduring resource that symbolized peace, civilization, and prosperity. The citizens, guided by wisdom and practicality, chose Athena's gift. This decision cemented her as the protector of the city, while Poseidon's pride and wrath remained, a reminder of the godly tension between creation and destruction, strategy and might.

The rivalry between Athena and Poseidon is emblematic of contrasting philosophies that echo in modern literature and contemporary thought. Athena represents calculated intelligence, diplomacy, and long-term planning—the virtues celebrated in heroes like Odysseus or modern figures in literature and politics who use strategy and foresight to achieve their goals. Poseidon, on the other hand, embodies elemental force, unpredictability, and emotional intensity—the raw power that can shape events through immediate action, much like the disruptive characters in contemporary novels or even real-world movements that challenge systems with sudden, forceful energy. Their contest illustrates the tension between measured wisdom and instinctual power, a dynamic still relevant in leadership, environmental debates, and societal decision-making today.

In literature and popular culture, the rivalry has inspired countless interpretations of wisdom versus power, intellect versus force, and civility versus chaos.

Contemporary novels, films, and even video games often explore similar dynamics: two opposing forces, each representing different strategies and values, clashing over control or influence. The Athena-Poseidon dichotomy is reflected in characters who must balance foresight and emotion, logic and instinct, or innovation and tradition. These stories remind readers that victory is often achieved not through sheer strength but through thoughtful, sustainable, and strategic action.

Ultimately, the rivalry between Athena and Poseidon is more than a tale of divine competition. It is a story about values, decision-making, and the balance between force and wisdom. It teaches that power without strategy can falter, while intellect without influence can be ignored. Their contest over Athens encapsulates a timeless lesson: civilizations—and individuals—flourish when wisdom guides action and when raw potential is tempered with insight. In modern times, as in ancient myth, the interplay between these forces continues to shape our understanding of leadership, creativity, and the human relationship with nature and society.

CHAPTER 5

Medusa: The Maiden Turned Monster

The first time we meet Medusa in the old Greek epics, she is already a monster—one of three Gorgon sisters, with hair of living snakes, a gaze that turns the unwary into stone. Her head is severed by the hero Perseus, a trophy for his quest, and eventually mounted on the goddess Athena's shield. In this telling, Medusa is not a person with a life or story—she is an obstacle, a danger, a thing to be overcome.

But that is only one version.

Later poets, particularly Ovid in *Metamorphoses*, gave her a backstory that turned the myth on its head. In Ovid's account, Medusa was once a mortal woman of remarkable beauty, her hair the envy of the world. She caught the attention of Poseidon, who pursued her and, in Athena's temple, violated her. Athena, enraged at the desecration of her sacred space—not at the perpetrator—punished

Medusa. The beautiful hair became serpents. Her gaze, once admired, became fatal.

This shift in the story is striking. It changes Medusa from a faceless monster into someone wronged, punished not for a crime she committed, but for what was done to her. In one sweep, the blame is relocated—not onto the god who harmed her, but onto the woman who endured it.

This dynamic is far from confined to myth. Across history, women have been punished not only for their perceived transgressions, but also for their survival of events beyond their control. In witch trials of medieval Europe, women who were widowed, outspoken, or simply different were branded as dangerous, accused of bringing misfortune to crops or community. In some colonial societies, women who resisted social constraints were cast as immoral or untrustworthy.

The pattern is hauntingly familiar: when something threatens the status quo—whether it is disaster, scandal, or a violation of sacred norms—the search begins for someone to bear the burden of blame. That someone is often a woman, her perceived "fault" magnified until she becomes, in the public mind, the cause of the harm.

Medusa's story, in this light, becomes a mythic case study in scapegoating. The transformation of her image—from a wronged mortal to a monstrous other—mirrors the way reputations can be rewritten to fit the needs of power. By making her the villain, the myth protects the image of the god, shields the sanctity of the temple, and upholds the heroic arc of Perseus.

In modern retellings—novels, films, poems—Medusa has been reclaimed as a symbol of female rage and survival. Artists imagine her not as a monster, but as a woman whose trauma was weaponized against her, her monstrous form a defense against further harm. To meet her gaze is not to be destroyed by evil, but to be confronted with the truth of what she endured.

The Greeks may have crafted her as an embodiment of divine punishment, but they also, perhaps unintentionally, left us a template for how injustice works:

1. Something happens that threatens order.
2. The real source of harm is too powerful or untouchable to blame.
3. A more vulnerable figure is chosen to carry the guilt.

4. That figure is remade in public perception—monster, witch, seductress—until the original story is forgotten.

When read through that lens, Medusa's face on Athena's shield takes on a different meaning. It is not merely a protective charm—it is a reminder of the costs of survival in a world that often blames the victim.

Today, we speak about "turning someone into a scapegoat" as if it were a modern political maneuver, but the roots run deep in our cultural stories. Medusa's myth shows how narratives are shaped to direct fear and anger away from the powerful and toward those least able to resist. Her petrifying gaze becomes a metaphor for the power such a falsely crafted image can have: once the story is set, it freezes perception in place.

And yet, the persistence of her myth into the modern era suggests that these narratives can also be reimagined. We can, if we choose, tell the story differently—restore Medusa's humanity, question the motives of her punishers, and see in her not a monster to be slain, but a survivor whose story was stolen.

CHAPTER 6
The Golden Apple of Discord

We all know the Trojan War to be the birthplace of eternal heroes like Achilles, Odysseus, and Ajax. It is a legend, famous for centuries as it explores universal themes of heroism, pride, glory, and the tragic costs of war. The iconic war made way for Homer's *Iliad* and *Odyssey*, which are the bedrocks of Western literature as we know it today.

The famous war's beginning is, like many other Greek stories, credited to the incessantly tumultuous squabbles of the Greek Gods themselves:

A magnificent feast was held on Mount Pelion at the celebrated wedding of King Peleus and sea-nymph Thetis, with a guest list including nearly all the Olympian Gods. The wedding was otherwordly–wedding presents included two immortal horses, a knife carved by Hephaestus himself, and a basket of "divine" irresistible salt. Eris, the Goddess of Discord, was one of the only Olympian Gods not invited to the wedding. Enraged, she threw an unwelcome wedding present into the celebration–her golden apple, inscribed with the words "to the fairest." Athena, Aphrodite, and Hera, consumed by vanity, scrambled to claim the golden apple as their own. Each believed they were the "fairest," or most beautiful, and therefore entitled to the prize.

Afraid of inciting conflict between the Gods, Zeus refused to choose the one deserving of the Golden Apple; instead, he appointed Paris, a Trojan prince known for his fairness, as judge. The three powerful goddesses each approached Paris with bribes. Hera offered Paris immense power and a chance to rule all of Asia and Europe. Athena bribed him with ultimate wisdom and the ability to defeat his enemies in battle. Aphrodite promised the love of Helen, admired across lands as the most beautiful woman in the world. Blind with longing, Paris chose Aphrodite to be awarded the Golden Apple, and was aided by Eros, Aphrodite's companion. Helen was already married to Menelaus, King of Sparta–and so, with Aphrodite's help, Paris seduced Helen and took her to Troy. Thus, the Trojan War began.

These themes, though wrapped in the robes of mythology, resonate powerfully in modern literature and culture. Margaret Atwood's *The Penelopiad* explores the *Odyssey* through Penelope's voice, illuminating how envy, rivalry, and desire ripple through human lives just as they did in the ancient world. In popular culture, the myth repeats itself endlessly—whether in films like *Mean Girls*, where a glittering plastic crown replaces the apple, or in reality television, where contestants sabotage each other for titles of beauty, fame, or love. Even in our digital age, social media platforms serve as a modern Mount Olympus, with "likes" and followers acting as golden apples tossed daily into the arena. The scramble for recognition, for being named "the fairest," is no less fierce now than it was on Olympus.

The Golden Apple, then, is more than a story about gods, mortals, and war. It is a parable of human nature, a reminder of how vanity, desire, and discord can unravel peace and lead to destruction. It is as relevant in our world of screens and selfies as it was in Homer's epics. The apple glitters still—not just in myth, but in every rivalry, every temptation, and every contest for validation we create.

CHAPTER 7
The Gods of Old

The Gods of old exist all around us. Their stories haunt the narratives of our favorite literature, become vibrant through the constellations in the night sky, and inspire authors and artists today.

If you look up at the night sky and see Orion, remember that he represents the mythical hunter Orion, doomed to be chased by the opposing constellation of the Scorpion as a consequence of his pride. Remember that the Greeks adapted and developed the Zodiac the next time you check your horoscope or ask a friend about their zodiac sign.

Remember the story of Orpheus and how he quite literally journeyed into Hell to retrieve his wife, Eurydice, who died on their wedding day. Remember that in every retelling of the story, Orpheus was granted permission to take her back from Hades, with the only condition that he could not look back to see her behind him–and that in every version of the tragic myth, Orpheus couldn't help but glance back, thus losing her forever. To love Eurydice is to look back–a love so legendary it is mythic.

Remember that when spring comes, it is a celebration of not just nature but of Persephone coming back home to her mother, Demeter, goddess of agriculture and fertility. Remember that the seasons exist because she was kidnapped by Hades, and her mother grieved so much that the harvest withered and the Earth became barren, thus giving way to the seasons of Fall and Winter. Remember that Zeus compromised to have Persephone spend six months with Hades and six months with her mother, demonstrating the duality between death/darkness and life/light.

Remember that Narcissus, consumed in vanity, brutally spurned all those that admired him; Nemesis, the goddess of retribution, lured him to a pool of water to enact her revenge. It was there that Narcissus saw his reflection for the first time, and in all his conceit, he fell in love with himself right then and there. Remember that Narcissus pined away for himself like others pined for him, eventually dying from his own vanity, and only a flower grew in his place.

Remember Icarus's fall–how Daedalus and his son Icarus devised wings to escape imprisonment on the island of Crete, but Icarus died because he did not heed the warnings of his father. Remember that his hubris became his downfall when he flew too close to the sun, but he was also warned not to fly too low as the seawater as it would weigh down his feathers.

Excessive pride has eternal consequences. Loving too much can prove to be self-destructive. Duality is necessary for balance. Vanity dooms people to be alone. Hubris kills, but complacency suffocates. These are the lessons Greek Mythology has taught generations. The myths of old endure because they remind us that the flaws of gods and mortals are more alike than different. In every age, the gods remind us that the battles between pride and humility, love and loss, excess and restraint, are not ancient—they are human.

www.ingramcontent.com/pod-product-compliance
Lightning Source LLC
Chambersburg PA
CBHW050025170726
48282CB00025B/550